COLLARED PECCARY–
THE JAVELINA

by Iona Seibert Hiser

Illustrated by Frank O'Leary

Steck-Vaughn Company • **Austin, Texas**

AN **Intext** PUBLISHER

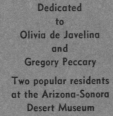

Dedicated
to
Olivia de Javelina
and
Gregory Peccary

Two popular residents
at the Arizona-Sonora
Desert Museum

Acknowledgments to:

Natie Gras, Director of the Animal Nursery for the Arizona-Sonora Desert Museum, for helpful information.

Hal Gras, Public Relations Director of the Arizona-Sonora Desert Museum, and also in charge of the Desert Ark, for his help.

Dr. Lyle K. Sowls, University of Arizona, and Director of the Arizona Cooperative Wildlife Research Unit, for his advice and helpful research material.

El Paso Zoological Gardens for assistance to the artist, Frank O'Leary.

Collared Peccary—The Javelina

When alarmed, the collared peccary
scoots away on small dark hoofs.
Scampering through the mesquite,
catclaw, and cactus of the southwestern
desert—or the scrub oak of low
mountains—it is soon out of sight.

Musk Gland

As the peccary flees, a strong musk
odor fills the air, an urgent warning to
others in the herd. The scent comes
from a musk gland on the animal's
slanting back, several inches above its
tail. When fright raises the long
bristling hair on the peccary's neck and
back, the musk gland opens to send forth
the far-reaching smell. This scent also
marks the herd's territory, leaving a
message that informs others they are
trespassing.

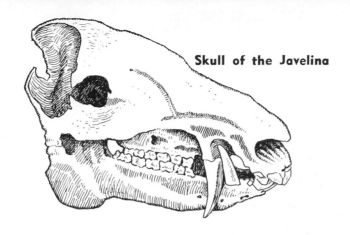

The Peccary's Family

Although the peccary is often called a "wild pig," it is not the same as the wild boars of Europe, Asia, North Africa, and the East Indies, and it is quite different from common domestic hogs. The javelina is a mammal that has belonged to a separate branch—the genus Tayassuidae (Tah-yass-swee-dee)—of the swine family for millions of years.

Peccaries have other names. The one most used in the Southwest is javelina (hav-vuh-lee-na), which comes from the Spanish word, jabalina, meaning a javelin or spear. The animal is called "javelina" because of its pointed, sharp tusks. The name collared peccary comes from its collar of whitish hair.

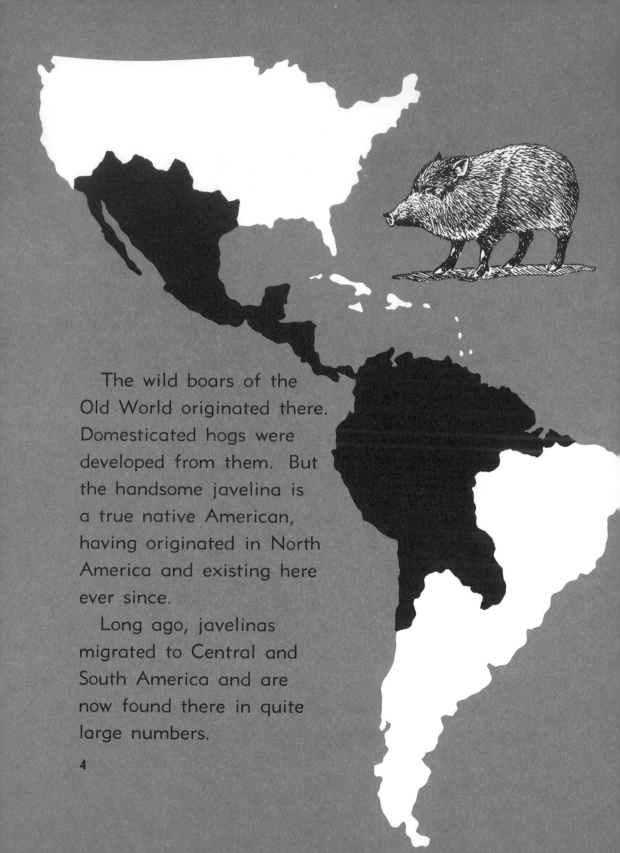

The wild boars of the Old World originated there. Domesticated hogs were developed from them. But the handsome javelina is a true native American, having originated in North America and existing here ever since.

Long ago, javelinas migrated to Central and South America and are now found there in quite large numbers.

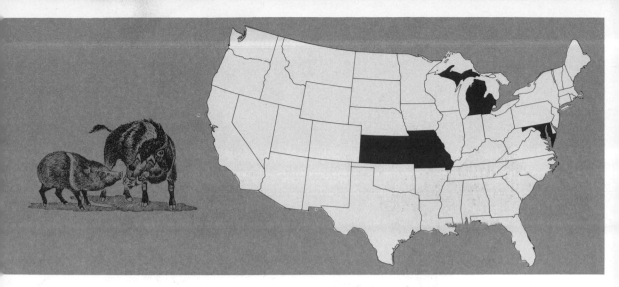

One prehistoric relative was an odd-looking, large peccary that once roamed parts of the United States. It had a long face with a large lump above each cheek, probably looking much like the wart hogs that now live in Africa.

Fossil bones of prehistoric peccaries have been unearthed in Missouri, Kansas, and as far east as Michigan and Maryland.

Today, there are only two species. The larger, very vicious, white-lipped peccary is found from Central Mexico southward. The little collared peccary lives in western and southern Texas, Arizona, southwestern New Mexico, Mexico, Central and South America.

European Wild Boar

Poland China Sow

Hippopotamus

Present Day Relatives

Besides the peccary's Old World wild relatives and its tame farm cousins, the hippopotamus also belongs to the swine family. More distant relatives, grouped together because they all belong to the even-toed order of split-hoofed animals, are sheep, goats, oxen, deer, camels, antelopes, and giraffes.

6

Kob (African Antelope)

Dromedary

Longhorn

Angora Goat

Giraffe

European Wild Boar

African Wart Hog

The Appearance of the Peccary

The javelina is smaller than European swine and African wart hogs. Males and females look alike except that the males usually are larger.

When grown, the collared peccary is from thirty-two to forty inches in length and from seventeen to twenty-three inches high at the shoulder. Peccaries seldom get fat. They work hard hunting food, and their weight depends partly on how much they find. Some adults weigh as little as thirty pounds; others, with abundant food, weigh more than fifty pounds.

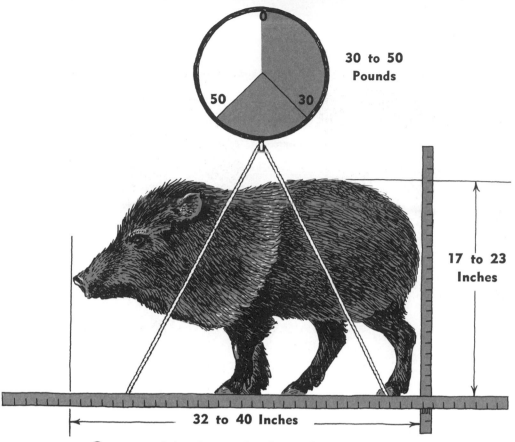

30 to 50
Pounds

17 to 23
Inches

32 to 40 Inches

Coarse, black-and-white banded bristles give the adults a pepper-and-salt look, the colors shading into black on the lower legs and into a darker streak down their backs. Around neck and shoulders the bristles are bushy and up to seven inches long, making the little animal's thick neck look even larger than it is.

The peccary's tail, little more than an inch long, is scarcely visible.

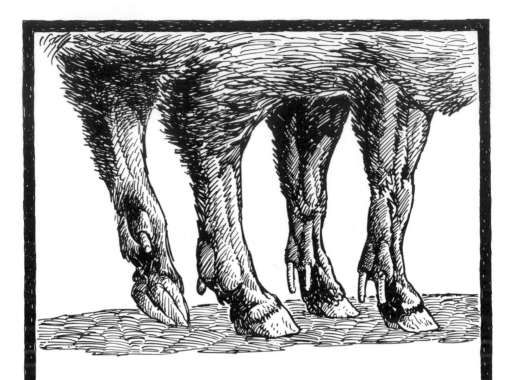

Like other split-hoofed animals, the
javelina walks on its toes. Its short
legs end in two large toes, each with a
complete hoof. The front feet also have
two dewclaws—tiny toes—about an inch
and a half above ground. The hind legs
have only one dewclaw each, high on the
inside. These little toes may help
support the weight when the owner wades
through deep mud.

The peccary's heavy head tapers to a
piglike, wiggly black snout, pinkish on
its flat end. With this, it roots in
the ground for bulbs, roots, and tubers.
Because the javelina's neck is so short,
it cannot reach to root very deeply
unless it drops to its front knees.
Often, the older adults have thick
calluses from so much kneeling.

The thick-lashed, shortsighted eyes
are pretty. Ears about four inches long
are set well back on the peccary's head
and are surrounded by long bristles.

When the javelina's mouth is open, its
thirty-eight teeth give it a fearsome
appearance, especially since the four
canines grow into straight, sharp-
pointed tusks several inches long. With
these weapons, the peccary can wound its
enemies.

The Sounds of the Peccary

When contented, the peccary repeats a soft, happy grunting. But if danger appears, a much deeper, louder "whoof!" of alarm is uttered as the group flees.

When hurt, the javelina makes piercing squeals. If angry, it gives shrill squeals of rage and clacks its big teeth together loudly, sounding like Spanish castanets. Sometimes the peccary whines and cries, but the "oink-oink" of the domestic pig is missing. If annoyed, peccaries often make a barking sound.

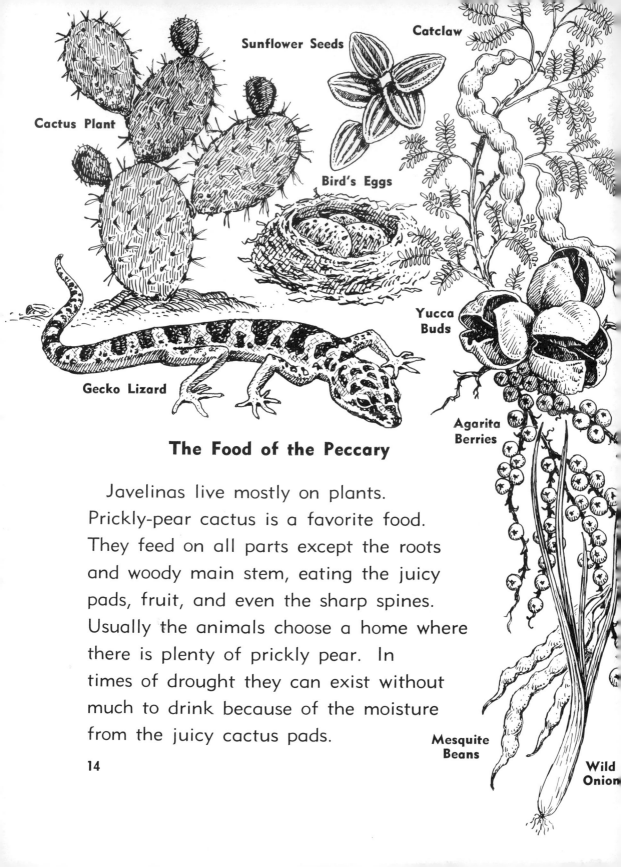

Cactus Plant

Sunflower Seeds

Catclaw

Bird's Eggs

Yucca Buds

Gecko Lizard

Agarita Berries

The Food of the Peccary

Javelinas live mostly on plants.
Prickly-pear cactus is a favorite food.
They feed on all parts except the roots
and woody main stem, eating the juicy
pads, fruit, and even the sharp spines.
Usually the animals choose a home where
there is plenty of prickly pear. In
times of drought they can exist without
much to drink because of the moisture
from the juicy cactus pads.

Mesquite Beans

Wild Onion

14

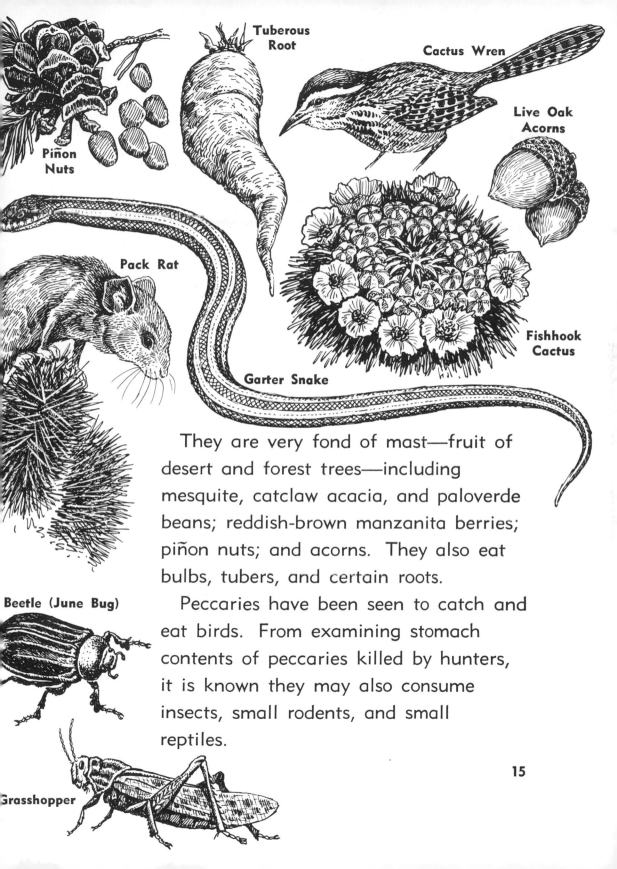

Piñon
Nuts

Tuberous
Root

Cactus Wren

Live Oak
Acorns

Pack Rat

Fishhook
Cactus

Garter Snake

Beetle (June Bug)

Grasshopper

They are very fond of mast—fruit of desert and forest trees—including mesquite, catclaw acacia, and paloverde beans; reddish-brown manzanita berries; piñon nuts; and acorns. They also eat bulbs, tubers, and certain roots.

Peccaries have been seen to catch and eat birds. From examining stomach contents of peccaries killed by hunters, it is known they may also consume insects, small rodents, and small reptiles.

15

Living Habits

Peccaries love company. Almost never found alone, they live together in herds that may have as few as five or as many as thirty-five members. Occasionally in winter they gather in larger groups of forty to fifty.

A javelina herd usually stays in a chosen locality the year around within a territory about three miles in diameter. Favorite living areas are low, rocky foothills near the base of a mountain range where the animals can find arroyos, caves, and crevices in which to hide during times of peril.

Both for food and for protection, they choose localities where mesquite, paloverde, catclaw, and plenty of cactus grow. When mast is ripe they leave the lower desert and ascend to higher regions among scrub oak and manzanita.

Traveling from one feeding spot to another, the peccaries often trot along single file.

As cold weather approaches, the peccary herds go back to lower elevations where the air is warmer, since they do not have a thick layer of fat to protect them in winter or a thick undercoat to help their coarse bristles keep them warm.

Peccaries feed mostly in the early
morning, late afternoon, and evening.
During the middle of the day they take a
rest—a siesta. In hot weather their
siesta is longer, and they feed more
during the coolness of night. When the
sun is high, they seek a cool spot near
the base of an overhanging cliff or in a
dense thicket and lie in their pawed-out
resting hollows.

18

On winter days when they feed longer,
their shorter rest period is taken lying
close together in the light shade of a
paloverde or some other desert growth.
During long winter nights, they sleep in
caves or old mine tunnels, huddled
snugly for warmth and grunting softly in
contented companionship.

Javelinas do not like storms and seek shelter in thick shrubbery or in a favorite tunnel or cave.

Sometimes a family squabble occurs, but it usually is settled quickly by snapping, barking, and a loud clacking of tusks.

Peccaries are clean and neat. Their bed hollows are kept free of soil.

Sight, Hearing, and Sense of Smell

Although javelinas are very nearsighted, their hearing is quite good, about equal to man's. Their sense of smell is highly developed. They locate certain underground bulbs just by keen sense of smell. A herd will root peacefully not far from some quiet observer—if the breeze is blowing the watcher's scent away. But if the wind shifts and blows from the man to the javelina, they quickly catch the human odor and dash away.

The Enemies of the Peccary

In spite of peccaries' sharp tusks
with which they can tear and slash, they
have enemies that prey on them. If a
javelina has a chance to run under a
thick, low bush or back into a crevice
for protection, it sometimes can fight
off a larger adversary, battling
viciously for its life. But a peccary
taken by surprise in open country by a
predator is apt to be killed.

Coyotes are one of the peccary's worst enemies. Their habit of hunting in teams makes it fairly easy for them to attack and bring down even an adult javelina.

The bobcat especially likes young peccaries. Sly and quiet, it easily creeps up on a baby peccary not well guarded by its mother.

Mountain lions are not much of a
threat because they usually do not
inhabit the same territory as peccaries.
But jaguars are sure death for them.

Even golden eagles are enemies. A
government trapper once saw two eagles
work as a team. The first eagle
attacked and sent the javelina rolling.
Before the animal could scramble to its
feet and try to fight, the second eagle
swooped down and killed it with its
fierce talons.

How Peccaries Rear Their Young

Baby peccaries can be born any season
of the year. The mother seeks shelter
in a cave or some other protected place.
Usually, there are just one or two young
peccaries, reddish-tan with a dark
stripe down their backs. A few months
later, the soft reddish hair is replaced
by the coarse black-and-white bristles.

26

When only a few hours old, the
peccaries can run around. A few days
after their birth, the mother takes her
young and rejoins the herd. Then the
babies are left to do as they please,
for the female javelina is not a very
good mother. She lets them nurse when
hungry, but pays scarcely any attention
to them as they romp and play. Javelina
mothers have been known to desert their
offspring when danger threatened.

Are Peccaries Dangerous to Man?

In the wild, peccaries usually prefer to run and get out of a human's way. Occasionally, one will stand its ground and clack its teeth threateningly. But a stone tossed in its direction will most likely drive a javelina away.

If found while very young, peccaries can be tamed and made into affectionate pets. But when grown, they cannot be fully trusted. Many of the pets have become mean—especially toward visitors. The most dangerous peccaries are the partly tame ones that have lost their fear of man. It is wise to stay at a safe distance from the unpredictable peccary.

Are Peccaries Harmful or Helpful?

Some ranchers fear that peccaries damage cattle country by rooting, but rooting kills a number of unwanted weeds, such as gourd vines, and also cultivates the soil, helping a grass crop to grow. Often javelinas are blamed for excavations made by skunks or other animals. Usually, the holes peccaries do make are leveled off by the next hard rain.

Now protected by law, javelinas may be hunted in season. Their meat makes good eating. The hides are manufactured into gloves, shoes, handbags, and other leather articles. Bristles can be used for brushes.

At one time, collared peccaries were in danger of becoming extinct. But now, protected, it is hoped these unusual animals may continue to thrive on the continents of the Americas.